A honeybee collecting pollen from a morning glory flower

Roses Red, Violets Blue

Why Flowers Have Colors

Sylvia A. Johnson

Photographs by
Yuko Sato

Lerner Publication Company ▪ Minneapolis, Minnesota

The publisher wishes to thank Peter D. Ascher, Professor of Horticultural Science, University of Minnesota, for his assistance in the preparation of this book.

All photographs by Yuko Sato with the exception of the following: p. 9, Masaharu Suzuki; p. 14, Nigel Harvey; p. 52, Minneapolis Public Library and Information Center.

Drawings by Hiromitsu Kamiyama.

Translation of original text by Wesley M. Jacobsen.

Library of Congress Cataloging-in-Publication Data

Johnson, Sylvia A.
    Roses red, violets blue: why flowers have colors / by Sylvia A. Johnson; photographs by Yuko Sato
      p.   cm.
    Text adapted from Colors of flowers and insects by Yuko Sato.
    Includes index.
    Summary: Examines the nature and function of flower colors and explains their role in attracting animal pollinators to help the plants reproduce.
    ISBN 0-8225-1594-6
    1. Flowers—Color. 2. Pollination by insects. [1. Flowers—Color. 2. Pollination.] I. Sato, Yuko, 1928-   . II. Sato, Yuko, 1928-   Colors of flowers and insects. III. Title
QK925.J64   1991
582.13′04463-dc20   90-27643
                                   CIP
                                   AC

Manufactured in the United States of America
2 3 4 5 6 7 8 9 10 99 98 97 96 95 94 93 92

Contents

This autumn garden is planted with golden marigolds, red salvia, and begonias in pink, rose, and white.

Introduction

Do you have flowering plants growing around your house? Maybe there is a garden in your backyard filled with irises and daylilies. Perhaps pots of deep purple African violets stand on the kitchen window sill, or bright red geraniums bloom on a sunny balcony or deck.

What is it about flowering plants that makes people love them so much and want to have them around? Some flowers have a sweet perfume that is pleasing to our sense of smell. Roses, lilacs, and lilies of the valley delight us with their wonderful fragrances. Other flowers have attractive forms and shapes. The simple cup of a tulip and the complicated structure of an orchid are fascinating to see and study.

Perhaps the feature of flowers that pleases people most is their color. Flowers come in an amazing variety of beautiful colors. Think of the glowing orange-red of a poppy or the soft lavender of lilacs. Blue flowers range from the deep indigo of some delphiniums to the pale blue of morning glories. Pink shades can be as vivid as a peony or as soft as an apple blossom. Flower colors include purples so dark that they look black and yellows so delicate that they are almost white.

Morning glories come in vivid shades of pink and purple as well as delicate blues and lavenders.

7

Speedwell flowers blooming in a meadow. Like all flowers, these fragile blossoms play an important role in the reproductive life of the plant.

With their appealing colors and fragrances, flowers have become an important part of people's lives. We sometimes forget that they are even more important in the lives of plants. Without flowers, many kinds of plants—trees and grasses as well as garden plants—would not be able to reproduce. The colorful petals of a flower surround and protect the reproductive parts of the plant. These parts produce the seeds from which new plants grow. And flower colors play an important role in the process by which seeds are produced.

Reproduction in the Plant World

Like all living things, plants survive on earth by producing more of their own kind. Some kinds of plants reproduce through **vegetative propagation**. This is a process in which new individuals develop from parts of an existing plant. Strawberry plants are produced on long stems called runners that are sent out by a parent plant. Potato plants can grow from a piece of a potato that includes an "eye," which contains the bud of a new plant.

Vegetative propagation produces new plants that are exactly the same as the plants from which they came. Another method of reproduction creates new individuals that are different from their ancestors. This method is known as **sexual reproduction**.

Like animals, many plants reproduce sexually. Sexual reproduction takes place through the union of male and female reproductive (sex) cells. This union creates a new being that is not exactly like either of its parents but combines some of their characteristics. Most plants, like most animals, benefit by the new combinations that result from sexual reproduction.

Sprouts growing from the "eye" of a potato. This form of reproduction produces a new plant exactly like its ancestor.

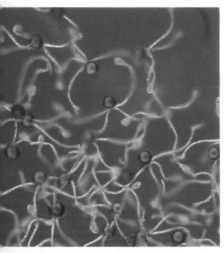

This photograph taken through a microscope shows the spores of a horsetail plant. Like ferns, horsetails produce spores as part of their reproductive process.

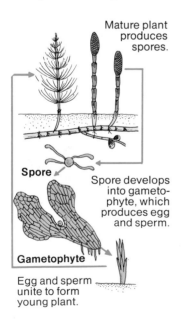

Mature plant produces spores.

Spore

Spore develops into gameto-phyte, which produces egg and sperm.

Gametophyte

Egg and sperm unite to form young plant.

Spore-producing Plants

Before we consider flowering plants, let's take a quick look at some other kinds of plants that reproduce sexually. Ferns and their relatives, the horsetails and club mosses, have a form of sexual reproduction that is different from that used by flowering plants. Instead of producing **seeds**, these plants produce small bodies called **spores**.

Spores are very different from seeds. A seed is a complex structure formed by the union of sex cells. Under the proper conditions, a seed will grow into a new plant. A spore develops not into a plant but into an in-between stage that produces male **sperm** and female **egg** cells. These sex cells then unite to form a new plant. (The diagram on this page shows the stages in the development of a horsetail from a spore to a new plant.)

In the fern family, **fertilization**—the union of egg and sperm—requires moisture. The tiny sperm can reach the egg cells only by swimming through water provided by rain or dew. Because of this requirement, ferns, horsetails, and club mosses grow best in damp climates or environments. If moisture is not present, their form of sexual reproduction cannot take place.

Conifers—"Naked-seed Plants"

Sexual reproduction in ferns does not involve flowers or seeds. Another group of plants, the conifers, reproduce without flowers, but they do have seeds.

Spores being released from the head of a horsetail plant

Female cones

Male cones

Ovules

Enlargement of female cone

Their seeds develop on the **cones** that give this group its name.

A conifer such as a spruce or pine has separate male and female cones that produce sex cells. The large female cones develop small structures called **ovules** on their scales. Egg cells grow inside the ovules. The smaller male cones produce **pollen**, a powdery substance made up of tiny grains that contain sperm.

Reproduction in conifers depends not on water but on the wind. The male cones release large amounts of pollen, and the wind carries some of the tiny grains to the female cones. This transfer of pollen is known as **pollination**.

When a pollen grain becomes caught in the sticky substance near an ovule opening, it develops a tube that goes down into the ovule. A sperm cell passes down the tube and unites with the egg cell. The ovule has now been fertilized and begins to develop into a seed.

Like the seed of a flowering plant, a conifer seed contains an **embryo**, or baby plant. It also contains food and other materials needed for the new plant's development.

Conifers are known as **gymnosperms**, or naked-seed plants, because their seeds develop on the surface of the cones. The seeds of flowering plants, as we shall see, develop deep inside the flowers. For this reason, flowering plants are called **angiosperms**, or enclosed-seed plants.

Right: *A cluster of male cones from a pine tree.* Above: *Pine pollen drifting on the wind. Like other conifers, pine trees depend on the wind to carry pollen from the male cones to the female cones.*

The rose is one of the most popular garden flowers. The different varieties of roses are famous for the beauty and fragrance of their blossoms.

Flowering Plants

The angiosperms first appeared on earth about 80 million years ago, near the end of the Mesozoic era. By the beginning of the Cenozoic era, 65 million years ago, flowering plants were thriving in most parts of the world. Since that time, trees, grasses, and thousands of other kinds of flowering plants have become the most important and most successful members of the plant kingdom.

What accounts for the success of flowering plants? Why have they dominated the plant world for the last 65 million years? To find answers to these questions, we need to look at the way in which flowering plants reproduce.

In many ways, the reproduction of flowering plants is similar to reproduction in other kinds of plants. Like ferns and conifers, flowering plants reproduce sexually, with new life being created by the union of male sperm and female egg cells. The sperm of a flowering plant is enclosed in a pollen grain, and the egg cell develops within an ovule. When egg and sperm join, a seed containing the embryo of a new plant begins to grow.

Despite these similarities, there are some important differences in the reproduction of flowering

Flowering plants include many important field crops as well as garden flowers. These bright yellow blossoms are the flowers of the rape plant, which is grown in Europe and Asia for its seeds.

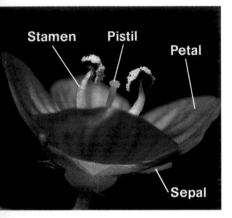

The Parts of a Flower

plants. Most of these differences have to do with the role of the flower in bringing male and female sex cells together.

What Is a Flower?

All the parts of a green plant have their special roles in the plant's life. Roots fasten the plant to the earth and take in water and minerals needed for survival. The stem contains tubes that carry water and other materials to all parts of the plant. The green leaves are food factories where the complicated process of **photosynthesis** takes place. And the flowers contain all the parts necessary for the plant's reproduction.

Although flowers vary greatly in their shapes, colors, and sizes, almost all have the same basic parts. At the base of most flowers is a set of green **sepals** that support and protect the colored **petals**. (In some flowers, the sepals are colored too.) The petals form a ring enclosing the parts of the flower that produce sex cells.

Many kinds of flowers have both male and female organs. The female organ, the **pistil**, is usually in the center of the flower. It is made up of three sections: a sticky knob, the **stigma**, which is connected by a stalk called the **style** to the sack-like **ovary**. It is within the ovary that ovules containing egg cells develop.

The **stamens**, the male organs of the flower, usually surround the pistil. Each stamen consists of a stalk called a **filament**, at the top of which is an **anther**.

16

Pollen containing sperm is produced by the anthers.

Although most flowers have both pistils and stamens, there are some that contain only one kind of reproductive organ. These flowers are known as **staminate** or **pistillate**, depending on whether they have male or female organs. In plants such as corn, both staminate and pistillate flowers grow on the same plant. Willows and some other trees have their male and female flowers on completely separate plants.

Pollination and Fertilization

The process of reproduction in a flowering plant begins with the transfer of pollen from the male stamens to the female pistil. When a pollen grain lands on the sticky stigma, it splits open and sends a tube down the style into the ovary. Sperm move down the tube, and one joins with an egg cell inside an ovule. The egg cell is now fertilized, and the ovule begins to develop into a seed.

Since most kinds of flowers have both male and female organs, you might think that pollination and fertilization would be simple. The pollen produced by a flower's stamens could easily reach the nearby pistil so that the sperm could fertilize the egg cells in the ovules. In fact, this process, known as **self-pollination**, does not often take place. **Cross-pollination**—the transfer of pollen from the stamens of one flower to the pistil of a flower on another plant—is more common.

If the male and female sex cells of the same flower

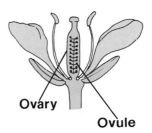

Ovules containing egg cells develop within the ovary of a flower. Some flowers have only one ovule, while others have hundreds or even thousands.

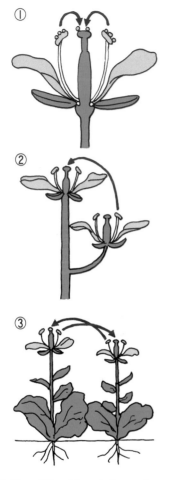

Self-pollination takes place when pollen is transferred from the stamens to the pistil of the same flower (1) or of another flower on the same plant (2). A flower is cross-pollinated when its pistil receives pollen from the stamens of a similar flower on another plant (3).

do join, the advantages of sexual reproduction may be lost. An egg and sperm produced by one flower will have much the same genetic material. A new plant created by a union of these cells will not have the variations that would exist if sex cells from two different plants had come together. Even different flowers on the same plant may produce sex cells that are quite similar in their genetic makeup.

To avoid the problems caused by self-pollination, plants have many ways of preventing a flower's pollen from reaching its own pistil. In many flowers, the male and female organs develop at different times. For example, the stamens may produce pollen at a time when the pistil is not able to receive it. Or the pistil may be **receptive** before pollen is produced. The sex organs of some flowers are positioned in such a way that pollen cannot easily reach the stigma of the pistil. The pistil, for example, may be tall while the stamens are short.

Since self-pollination is not very common in flowering plants, how is pollen usually transferred from flower to flower? Plants cannot move, so they cannot do the job themselves. In some plants, wind is the agent that carries pollen from stamens to pistils. In a great many plants, animals perform the job of pollination.

Animal Messengers

Animal pollinators include birds, bats, and even mice, but the great majority are insects. Bees, but-

Male flower

Female flower

The hop plant (left) is pollinated by the wind. Like many wind-pollinated plants, it has separate male and female flowers (above). Female hop flowers are among the ingredients used in making beer.

terflies, and moths head the list of insects that transfer pollen from the stamens of one flower to the pistils of other similar flowers.

Of course, these insects do not know that they are serving as pollen-carriers. When they visit flowers, they are looking for food: the sweet nectar hidden deep inside as well as the golden pollen on the anthers. But flowers are made in such a way that an insect visitor usually cannot avoid picking up pollen and carrying it away. Flower structures also make

A swallowtail butterfly drinking nectar from the flower of a cherry tree. In its search for food, the insect picks up pollen and carries it to other cherry blossoms.

sure that the pollen will eventually be delivered to the receptive stigma of another flower.

Flowers and insects work together in some amazing ways to make pollination possible. But before pollination can take place, insects must first find the flowers. Odor is one of the means by which flowers attract insects. The sweet fragrances that humans find so pleasing also appeal to bees and moths.

Another important way in which flowers attract insects is through color. The luscious colors of flower petals exist not to please human viewers but to send messages to insects. Most of these messages are related to the all-important subject of reproduction.

3

Why Flowers Have Colors

The colors of flowers, like many of the colors that we see in the natural world, are created by a very complicated process. They are produced when light strikes different **pigments**, natural coloring materials contained within flowers petals and other objects.

Light is one of the forms of **electromagnetic radiation** that comes from the sun and travels through space in waves. Light from the sun usually looks white to human eyes, but it is actually made up of many different colors. When a beam of sunlight passes through a special piece of glass known as a prism, you can see these colors. They make up what scientists refer to as the **visible light spectrum**. The rainbows created when sunlight passes through drops of water in the atmosphere also reveal the beautiful colors of the spectrum.

The colors of the visible spectrum are produced by light of different wavelengths. At one end of the spectrum are very short wavelengths that appear as violet. The long wavelengths at the other end of the visible spectrum are seen as red.

The yellow color of the rape flower is created by pigments that reflect certain wavelengths of light.

Visible Light Spectrum

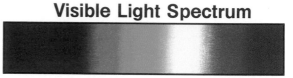

Violet Indigo Blue Green Yellow Orange Red

Left: *This photograph shows two rainbows produced by sunlight passing through drops of water on a spider's web. The colors of the rainbow make up what scientists call the visible light spectrum.*

Pigments cause objects to appear colored by absorbing some wavelengths of light and reflecting others. When sunlight strikes a flower or other object containing a yellow pigment, for example, the pigment absorbs all the wavelengths in the spectrum *except* those that produce yellow. These wavelengths are reflected by the pigment. When the wavelengths strike the eyes of humans and some other animals, they set off a reaction that causes the object to appear yellow.

Pigments in Flowers

Flowering plants contain several different kinds of pigments that play vital roles in the plants' lives. The most important plant pigment is **chlorophyll**, which produces the green color of plant leaves and stems. Chlorophyll is also one of the key elements in the food-making process of photosynthesis. By absorbing sunlight, this pigment supplies the energy that makes photosynthesis possible.

Chlorophyll is found in plant leaves, stems, and sepals, but not usually in flowers. The beautiful and varied colors of flowers are created by different kinds of pigments contained in the cells of the petals. Some colors are produced by only one pigment, while others are due to a combination of pigments. All these wonderful colors exist only because of the remarkable way in which the eyes and brain of a viewer react to the light waves reflected by the different pigments.

This cross-section photograph shows the green pigment chlorophyll contained within the cells of a leaf.

Many plants contain anthocyanin pigments. These coloring agents produce the beautiful rosy red of the garden balsam (right). The dark reds of maple leaves in autumn (above) are also due to anthocyanin pigments.

Red, Purple, Blue: The Versatile Anthocyanin Pigments

Many flowers have petals in different shades of red, pink, purple, and blue. Scarlet geraniums, blush-pink peonies, royal-blue delphiniums, and deep purple pansies are only a few of the flowers that display these elegant tints. All these colors are created by a group of pigments known as **anthocyanins.**

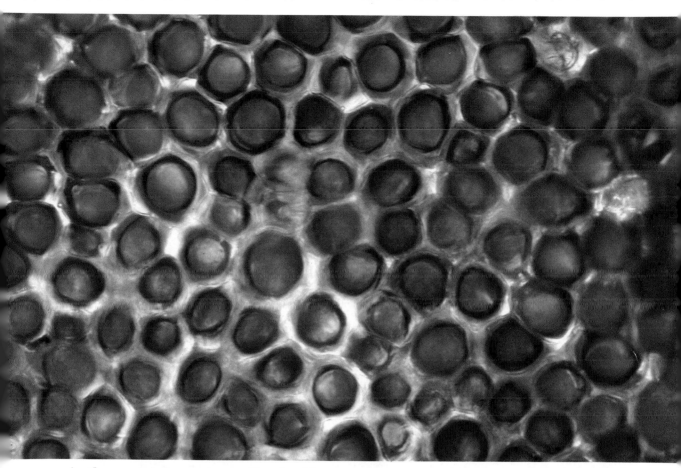

Anthocyanin pigments are dissolved in the sap of plant cells (above). In some flowers like the garden balsam, the pigments are found only in the outer layers of cells (right).

25

A vivid pink morning glory (above) and a deep blue dayflower (below) both contain varieties of anthocyanin pigments.

The anthocyanins are very common pigments in the plant world. Many fruits, among them apples, plums, and strawberries, owe their colors to these pigments. The vivid red of some autumn leaves is also due to anthocyanin pigments, which appear when the green chlorophyll is no longer being produced.

Unlike other plant pigments, the tiny particles that make up anthocyanin pigments are able to mix with liquids. In flowers, they are found dissolved in the sap contained within the individual cells of the petals. In some flowers, all the cells of the petals contain the coloring material, while in others, it appears only in the outer layers of cells.

The anthocyanin pigments that produce reds, blues, and purples are very closely related to each other. This is the reason that some species of flowers —for example, delphiniums—have red, blue, and purple varieties, but not orange and yellow ones. Some of the variations in anthocyanin colors are caused by the chemical composition of the cell sap in different plants. Sap with a high degree of acid in it will cause anthocyanin pigments to appear pink or reddish. Alkaline sap produces purplish or bluish tones.

You can try a simple experiment that demonstrates how the color of anthocyanin pigments can change. All you need are a few flowers with deep purple or bluish-purple petals and some materials that you probably have around the house. The instructions for the experiment are given on page 28.

Hydrangeas are familiar garden flowers that exhibit the changeable nature of anthocyanin pigments. The colors of the blossoms are affected by the chemical composition of the soil in which the plants grow. By adding a chemical like lime to the soil, gardeners can change blue hydrangeas (right) to pink ones (above). Other chemicals cause pink flowers to become blue.

Experimenting with Anthocyanin Pigments

Materials needed

1/2 cup water
White vinegar (acid)
Baking soda (alkaline)
Large glass measuring cup
2 small glass or pottery bowls
Medicine dropper
Teaspoon
Microwave oven
Several flowers with dark purple or bluish-purple petals.
We used cineraria (right), a potted flowering plant. Pansies
or irises from the garden would also be good choices.

Note: If you don't have a microwave oven, see the directions
on the next page.

1. Put 1/2 cup water in measuring cup.
Place in microwave oven and bring to a
vigorous boil.

2. Remove cup and put petals torn from
flowers into water (A). Return to microwave and continue boiling for 1 to 3
minutes. The boiling process will extract
the anthocyanin pigments from the flower
petals (B).

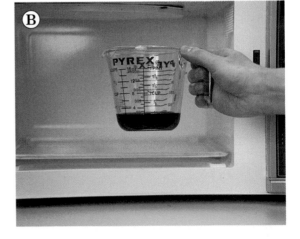

3. Take the cup out of the microwave and use a spoon to remove flower petals. Notice how the color has been stripped from the petals.

4. After the liquid has cooled a little, pour into the two small bowls.

5. Begin adding vinegar a drop at a time to one bowl (C). The acid in the vinegar should cause the bluish color to gradually become more red (D, E).

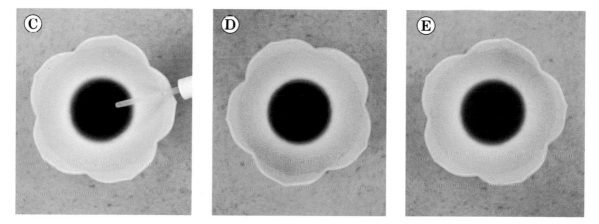

6. Now add a spoonful of baking soda to the liquid in the other bowl (F) and stir until it is dissolved. The alkaline soda will make the pigments a deeper blue (G, H).

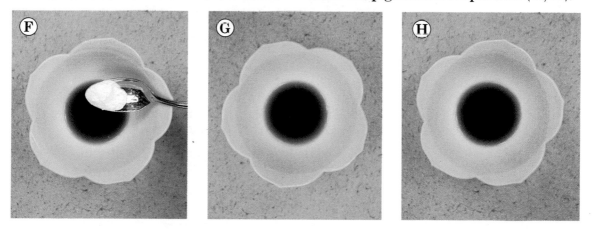

If you don't have a microwave, you can boil the flower petals in a pan on the stove. After removing the petals, pour the liquid into two small bowls and continue the experiment from Step 5.

The yellow color of dandelions (above) and rape flowers (right) is produced by carotene pigments.

Carotenes: The Pigments of Dandelions, Daffodils—and Carrots

Another important group of plant pigments are the **carotenes**. Carotene pigments, along with their close relatives the **xanthophylls**, are responsible for many of the yellow and orange colors in flowers and other plant parts. These pigments also play a role in photosynthesis, helping chlorophyll to use the energy of the sun in producing food.

Unlike the anthocyanin pigments, carotenes are

not dissolved in a plant's cell sap. Instead they are enclosed in **plastids**, small structures found in the part of the cell called the **cytoplasm**. This is the area where many of the important activities of the cell take place.

Within a plant's leaves, carotenes and xanthophylls occur in plastids along with the green pigment chlorophyll. Because these plastids contain chlorophyll, they are known as **chloroplasts**. In petals and other flower parts such as anthers and pistils, the yellow and orange pigments alone are found in plastids called **chromoplasts**.

Carotene pigments contribute to photosynthesis by helping chlorophyll to trap and hold the energy of the sun. In their role as coloring materials, they produce many of the orange, red-orange, gold, and yellow colors of flowers. Spring daffodils owe their color to carotenes, as do the pesky dandelions that pop up in smooth green lawns. Other yellow and orange flowers like marigolds contain xanthophyll pigments.

Carotene pigments are also very common in vegetables. Carrots contain large amounts of carotenes. In fact, the pigments were first identified in this food plant and named after it. The orange colors of cantaloupes and sweet potatoes are also due to carotene pigments. Egg yolks and butter get their color from the carotenes contained in the green parts of plants eaten by chickens and cows. When people eat animal or plant foods containing carotenes, their

The petals of this marigold contain xanthophyll pigments. Like the carotenes, these pigments are enclosed in chromoplasts, tiny bodies within a flower's cells (below).

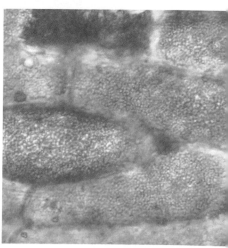

bodies can convert the pigments into Vitamin A, a very important nutrient.

What Produces the "Colors" of White and Black Flowers?

Although some flowers appear to be either snowy white or inky black, this appearance may be deceiving.

Some flowers that seem to be white are actually a very pale yellow or cream, due to the presence of small amounts of xanthophyll pigments. Other flowers look white because of the physical structure of their petals. Air spaces in the cells of the petals reflect the light waves that strike the flower. When all the wavelengths of the visible spectrum are reflected equally and none is absorbed, an object appears white. This kind of reflection is also what causes snow to look white to our eyes.

Many "black" flowers—for example, exotic varieties of tulips—are actually a very deep purple that is produced by anthocyanin pigments. Other black plant colors may be caused by the combined effect of different pigments such as purple anthocyanin and green chlorophyll. The physical structure of a flower may also give it a blackish appearance. If the texture or some other feature of the flower causes it to absorb all the wavelengths of visible light, then the flower may look black. This is the opposite of the complete reflection of light waves that produces white.

The white color of this tulip is not due to pigments but to the physical structure of its petals (top). The petals contain air spaces that reflect light waves. When an object reflects all the light waves of the visible spectrum, our eyes see it as white.

Studying Plant Pigments

Scientists have studied pigments closely in order to learn about their makeup and their roles in the lives of plants. They have discovered many fascinating things.

One thing that scientists have learned is the importance of light in the development of some plant pigments. Experiments with young plants raised in the dark, for example, have shown that the blue, purple, and red anthocyanin pigments will not appear without the presence of light. Chlorophyll is

Left: *The bud of a spiderwort flower cut open early in its development. The stamens are yellow, but the petals and other flower parts are colorless.* Center: *As the spiderwort continues to grow, light reaches the bud and causes its anthocyanin pigments to turn purple.* Right: *A spiderwort flower in full bloom. A bee is taking pollen from its yellow anthers.*

Left: *This photograph shows a hyacinth plant grown in a dark room. Its leaves are yellow instead of green, and its flower buds are without color.* Center: *Three hours after the plant was put in sunlight, its leaves began to turn green.* Right: *After three days in the sun, the hyacinth plant's leaves are dark green and its flowers are purple.*

another pigment that depends on light for its development. The leaves of a plant kept in a dark room will be yellow instead of green.

The yellow leaves of a plant deprived of light suggest something very interesting. Yellow pigments do not seem to need light for their development. Scientific studies have shown that this is true. The yellow carotene and xanthophyll pigments that are associated with chlorophyll appear even when a plant is kept in the dark. Without chlorophyll, of course, the plant cannot produce food through photosynthesis. A plant deprived of light will eventually die.

Yellow pigments not only develop without chlorophyll, but they also survive after the green pigment in a plant is gone. This is the reason that the leaves of many plants become yellow in the autumn.

As the growing season comes to an end, a plant stops producing the green chlorophyll that gave its leaves their characteristic color. With the chlorophyll gone, the carotene and xanthophyll pigments can be seen. These yellow and orange pigments were always in the cells of the leaves, but they were hidden by the intense green of chlorophyll.

The disappearance of chlorophyll in autumn is only one of the many changes that take place in pigments during the lives of plants. We have seen how the colors of hydrangeas change depending on the chemical composition of the soil. Other flowers change colors naturally over time. Some evening primrose, for example, are a bright yellow when they open during the evening hours. By morning, when the blossoms wither and die, they have changed to gold. Morning glory flowers change even more, sometimes going from blue to purple to red during their brief lives.

Scientists who have studied such color changes tell us that they can be caused by many different things. One of the causes is an increase in the amount of pigment that a flower contains. A yellow flower

Above: *A cross-section photograph of a leaf showing the green pigment chlorophyll in its cells.* **Below:** *As chlorophyll disappears at the end of the growing season, the orange carotene pigments in the cells are revealed.*

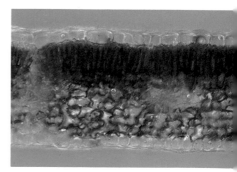

35

This evening primrose is yellow when it opens during the evening hours (left). The next morning, the flower has withered and its color has changed to an orange-gold (right).

manufactures more and more carotene pigment during its life. The older the flower is, the more pigment it has in its cells. This is why a yellow evening primrose may change to a deep gold before the flower wilts and dies.

Other color changes take place in response to pollination and fertilization. After the egg cells in the ovules are fertilized, all the nutrients in the flower are sent to the ovary to help in its development. This drastic change in the flower's chemistry affects anthocyanin pigments, causing them to change in color and to fade. This kind of color change may send a message to animal pollinators, telling them that the flower has already been pollinated and that they do not need to visit it.

The Messages Sent by Flowers

The colors of flowers, as well as their shapes, markings, and odors, all play a part in the complicated process that makes pollination possible. The key to the process is cooperation between plants and their animal pollinators. By means of this partnership, both plants and animals get just what they need.

What Animals Get from Pollination

It is clear how plants benefit from pollination. But what do most animals get out of the process that makes their efforts worthwhile? Food is the answer. Many insects—butterflies, moths, and particularly bees—receive almost all their food from flowers.

Most adult butterflies and moths eat nectar, the sugary liquid produced in the parts of flowers known as **nectaries**. All the members of a honeybee colony get their nourishment from flower products. Developing young bees eat the pollen brought back to the hive by adult worker bees. The adults drink nectar from flowers and also carry the sweet liquid to the hive to be stored. When nectar is mixed with

A cabbage butterfly drinks nectar from a rape flower.

A honeybee taking pollen from a fleabane flower. The insect has already collected a load of golden pollen in its "pollen basket," a hollow area on the rear leg. In the circle is a closeup photograph of an empty pollen basket.

enzymes produced by the worker bees' bodies, it becomes honey, a food that keeps well and is a good source of energy.

Many birds that pollinate flowers also feed on nectar. This high-energy food provides nourishment for quick-moving birds like the American hummingbirds or the sunbirds of Africa and Asia. A hummingbird may consume as much as twice its own weight in nectar every day.

Pollen is available as a food because plants manufacture it as part of their reproductive process. In order to feed the pollinators, a plant simply produces more pollen than it needs for reproduction. Nectar, on the other hand, plays no role in a plant's own life. This sweet liquid is produced solely to tempt insects and other animals into flowers so that they can pick up pollen.

How Animals and Flowers Get Together

Animals are attracted to flowers by many things, but one of the most important is color. The color of a flower often determines which animal will find it and how successful the pollinator will be in doing its job.

There are some general rules about the role of flower colors in attracting pollinators. Brightly colored flowers tend to appeal to animals active in the daytime. Bees, butterflies, beetles, and birds usually look for flowers with blue, pink, purple, yellow, or red petals that are conspicuous under the daytime sun.

At night, these bright colors are useless in attracting pollinators. Flowers that are pollinated by night-flying animals like moths and bats are often white or some very light color. Their pale petals stand out against the darkness, making them easy for pollinators to see. Many night-blooming flowers, for example, honeysuckles, also have a strong odor that attracts animals looking for food.

Daytime pollinators are attracted to bright colors, but they have even more specific color preferences. For example, bees are attracted to blue and yellow flowers, while birds like red flowers. Many bright red flowers such as the cardinal flower are pollinated exclusively by hummingbirds. Very few insects, however, are attracted to pure red flowers.

What is it about red that makes it attractive to birds but unappealing to most insects? Scientists

Many daytime pollinators like this butterfly are attracted to bright colors.

Flowers that bloom at night are often white so that they can be easily seen by pollinators. This exotic white flower is from a snake gourd plant.

who have studied this question have come up with a surprising answer. While birds notice red objects in much the same way that humans do, bees and many other insects cannot see red.

How Insects See Colors

It is difficult for people to understand why insects cannot see the vivid reds that are so obvious to us. Part of the problem is that we think of colors as having their own existence. In fact, they exist only as a response of our eyes and brains to the reflection of certain wavelengths of light. Animals with different eyes and brains will not necessarily have the same response or "see" the same colors.

Scientists have studied the color vision of animals and have discovered some fascinating things. For example, many animals are not sensitive to colors at all. Dogs and cats see mainly shades of grey in their world. On the other hand, apes, monkeys, and many kinds of birds seem to have a color vision similar to that of humans.

Research has shown that while many insects see colors, their color vision is not the same as ours. The eyes of an insect like the honeybee are sensitive to slightly different wavelengths of light than human eyes are. A bee's visible spectrum does not include most of the long wavelengths that cause

Although many insects notice pinkish-red flowers like these rhododendron blossoms, very few can see pure red flowers.

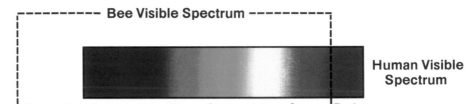

Bee Visible Spectrum

Human Visible Spectrum

Ultraviolet   Violet   Indigo   Blue   Green   Yellow   Orange Red

Bees and other insects cannot see red, but their eyes are sensitive to reflected ultraviolet light. This light lies beyond the violet end of the human visible light spectrum and is invisible to our eyes.

humans (and birds) to see red. On the other hand, bees and many other insects respond to some of the very short wavelengths beyond the violet end of the human visible spectrum. They can actually see reflected **ultraviolet** radiation.

Human eyes are not sensitive to the waves of ultraviolet radiation that come from the sun. (This form of electromagnetic radiation affects us most directly by causing sunburn.) For insects, however, ultraviolet is one of the colors in the visible light spectrum. A bee sees ultraviolet just as distinctly as a person sees red.

Scientists describe an insect's visible spectrum as "shifted" toward the ultraviolet, compared to the visible spectrum of humans. This means not only that many insects can see ultraviolet and not see red, but also that some of the other colors they see are different than the ones we know.

Pure yellow flowers, for example, probably look the same to a person and a bee since the eyes of both are sensitive to wavelengths in this part of the visible spectrum. Flowers that are white to humans, however, are apparently not white to bees. Flowers look white to us because they reflect all the colors of the visible spectrum, including red. But red is not part of a bee's visible spectrum. Therefore, flowers that reflect red are not "perfect reflectors" to a bee.

Most flowers that are white to humans probably appear blue-green to bees because these are the wavelengths (other than red) that they reflect most prominently.

Insects also see colors that result from a combination of ultraviolet with other wavelengths of light, for example, ultraviolet and yellow. Scientists who study insect vision give these special colors names like "bee-purple" to suggest how different they must be from the colors that we see.

Seeing Ultraviolet

It is difficult to imagine exactly how flower colors look to insects since their color vision is so different from ours. With the help of special photographic equipment, however, it is possible to get some idea of how bees and other insects see ultraviolet.

Scientists studying flower colors have taken photographs using special lenses and filters that are sensitive to reflected ultraviolet light. These photographs reveal many remarkable things. For example, some flowers that look plain yellow or white to human eyes actually have distinctive markings that reflect ultraviolet light. These markings are normally invisible to us but can easily be seen by bees and other insects.

What role do these ultraviolet markings play in the process of pollination? Most scientists think that they serve as signposts pointing an insect toward the part of the flower where pollen and nectar can

A photograph of a fleabane flower taken with ordinary black-and-white film.

This photograph of the same flower taken with special film and lenses shows ultraviolet light reflected from the outer petals.

A dandelion (left) usually looks plain yellow to human eyes. In a black-and-white photograph (center), the flower also shows little variation. But an ultraviolet photograph (right) reveals a strong contrast between the inner and outer sections. This difference helps to direct insects to the center part of the flower, where pollen and nectar can be found.

A butterfly locates the nectar in the center of a rape flower (above) by following the ultraviolet markings, which are clearly revealed in this special photograph (right).

be found. In flowers that look solid white or yellow to us, the ultraviolet markings often produce a contrast between the outer ring of petals and the center of the flower. In the center, of course, are located the stamens with their supplies of golden pollen. Ultraviolet markings also help to direct a bee or butterfly to the nectaries filled with sweet nectar.

Pointing the Way to the Nectar

Nectaries are located in different parts of flowers, and they are usually well hidden. They are often found deep in a flower's throat or in special structures called **spurs**. Insects have to work hard in order to reach the precious nectar. But flowers provide plenty of signs so that the pollinators can find the way.

Many flowers have patterns of lines or spots on their petals called **nectar guides**. These patterns actually point to the part of the flower where the nectaries are located. When an insect lands on a flower petal, all it has to do is follow the dotted line in order to get its sweet reward.

People can see the nectar guides of some flowers. They are in colors that, at least to human eyes, contrast with the color of a flower's petals. For example, irises often have black, brown, or yellow stripes that indicate where nectaries are located. In addition to these obvious marks, many flowers have ultraviolet nectar guides that are visible only to insects. These secret roadsigns point the way to the nectar just as clearly as the marks that humans can see.

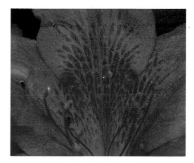

Nectar guides in a rhododendron flower lead a honeybee to the tube-shaped nectary deep inside the flower's throat.

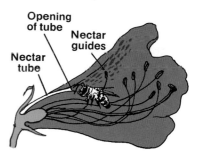

Opening of tube

Nectar guides

Nectar tube

The evening primrose is a night-blooming flower that opens in the evening and closes the following morning. It is pollinated not only by night-flying animals like moths but also by bees that come in the early morning, while the flower is still open (above). To attract these daytime pollinators, the evening primrose has ultraviolet nectar guides (left). The center of the flower absorbs ultraviolet light, while the outer parts reflect it. This contrast clearly points the way to the nectar and pollen.

The Right Shape for the Right Pollinator

When an insect follows a flower's nectar guides to the store of sweet nectar, it is also following the path that leads to pollination. In reaching the nectar, a pollinator usually picks up pollen from the flower's anthers or deposits pollen on its stigma. But not just any pollinator can take nectar from a flower and serve as the means of transferring its pollen. Just as the colors of flowers attract specific animals, so do their shapes and structures.

A flower with a simple, open shape like the speedwell may be pollinated by several kinds of insects.

Some flowering plants are not very choosy about their pollinators. Flowers like poppies or water lilies, which have a simple, open shape, can be pollinated by many kinds of insects, beetles and flies as well as bees. These simple flowers often do not produce nectar. They offer only pollen as a reward to visiting animals.

Flowers that produce nectar have evolved many complicated shapes to protect their valuable product and to make sure that it gets to the right animals. Often the petals of these flowers are joined to form bells, funnels, or tubes, with the nectaries hidden deep inside. Animals that pollinate the flowers must be able to reach down inside them to get to the nectaries. The most important equipment they need to achieve this goal is a long tongue.

Insects such as beetles, flies, and ants do not have long tongues, but many other kinds of insects do. A bee has a tube-shaped mouth structure, called a **proboscis**, with a long tongue inside it. Pushing its

The long, narrow tube of a honeysuckle requires a pollinator with a long tongue. Night-blooming honeysuckles like the white variety shown here are often pollinated by moths. Hummingbirds pollinate some red honeysuckles that are open during the day.

proboscis down into the throat of a flower like a petunia, a bee sucks up nectar with its tongue. Butterflies and moths have even longer proboscises, so long that they are kept coiled up when not in use. Flowers pollinated by these insects—for example, phlox—often have deep, narrow throats.

Flowers with tubes too deep and narrow even for butterflies and moths are often just right for hummingbirds. Many of these small birds have long, slender beaks containing even longer tongues. Hovering in the air near a flower like the red honeysuckle, a hummingbird thrusts its tongue into the narrow tube and sucks up nectar. In the process, it picks up pollen on its feathered head or breast.

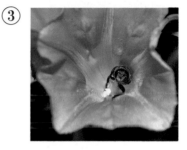

(1) Groundsel is a **composite flower** made up of many individual parts called **florets.** In the center is a cluster of tube-shaped florets containing the nectaries and reproductive parts. The outer "petals" are ray florets that attract insects and provide a landing platform for them. Composite flowers are usually pollinated by bees and butterflies, which are able to reach into the narrow tube florets with their long tongues.

(2) The thistle is another composite flower. Unlike the groundsel and its relatives, it is made up only of tube florets. Bees looking for nectar probe into the small, narrow tubes and, in the process, pollinate the flowers.

(3) Morning glories are shaped like wide funnels. Bees and other small insects can crawl into these flowers to find the nectaries. Other flowers like the bluebell have their funnels facing downward.

(4) The petals of the catchfly are joined at the base to form a long, thin tube. To reach the flower's nectar, insects have to push their tongues down inside the tube.

(5) A jewelweed flower stores its nectar in a spur (indicated by arrow). When a bee crawls into the flower to get to the nectar, it picks up pollen on its back.

Because butterflies perch on flowers while drinking nectar (above), the flowers they pollinate have to provide some kind of landing platform. Moths usually hover in the air while feeding (right).

Other characteristics of flowers are suited to particular kinds of pollinators. Bees and butterflies usually land on flowers in order to take nectar and pollen. The flowers they pollinate have to provide the insects with a place to perch or cling. Some of these flowers, for example, snapdragons, have extended petals that serve as "landing platforms" for the insect visitors. Moths, unlike their relatives the butterflies, do not usually perch while drinking nectar. Because moths hover in the air while feeding, the flowers they pollinate do not need landing platforms.

Traps and Tricks Used by Flowers

Some flowers use unusual methods to make sure that insects pick up pollen and carry it away with them. Many flowers in the pea family have their pistils, stamens, and nectaries enclosed within two petals joined together to form a **keel**. When an insect lands on the keel, its weight should force the petals to open and uncover the enclosed parts. If the insect is not heavy enough, however, it will not be able to reach the pollen and nectar.

The many kinds of orchids are noted for the surprising ways in which they achieve pollination. Most orchids produce pollen in tiny clusters called **pollinia**. Held together by sticky or waxy substances, the pollinia contain thousands of pollen grains.

When an insect like a wasp or bee searches for nectar within an orchid's complicated structure, it is often forced against the pollinia. It ends up with the little golden clusters stuck to its head or body, like a strange kind of ornament. When the insect moves on to another orchid, the pollinia come in contact with its stigma, and pollination takes place.

Orchids in a group called *Ophrys* have a system of pollination that is almost too fantastic to believe. These exotic flowers are mimics, resembling the females of certain species of wasps and bees. They are pollinated by male insects that are trying to mate with them!

Ophrys orchids not only look like female insects, but they also smell like them. The flowers produce a

The milk vetch is a member of the pea family. Its reproductive parts are enclosed in a keel (indicated by arrow) that must be forced open by a pollinating insect.

51

The complicated structure of an orchid is designed to make sure that a pollinator comes in contact with the flower's clusters of pollen.

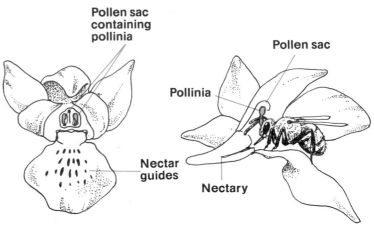

Pollen sac containing pollinia

Pollen sac

Pollinia

Nectar guides

Nectary

ORCHID FROM FRONT

CROSS-SECTION VIEW

fragrance that is exactly like the odor produced by females when they are ready to mate. Attracted by this odor, a male wasp or bee grabs onto an orchid just as he would a mate. Of course, the insect is not able to mate with the orchid, but during the attempt, he gets the flower's pollinia attached to his body. When he flies off to another orchid, he takes the pollinia with him.

This system of pollination works because there are usually no female insects around to compete with the orchids. In these species, the females develop later than the males. By the time that the females are ready to mate, the frustrated male insects have already pollinated many orchids.

This bee has just visited an orchid and has come away with the pollinia attached to its head. The photograph was taken while the bee was searching for nectar in another kind of flower.

Sometimes animals get the rewards of pollination without actually doing the work. An insect like this hornet (below) may bite a hole in the outside of a flower and drink nectar through it. Once the hole is made, other insects take advantage of it, and the flower may never be pollinated. Beetles sometimes eat the whole flower, petals and all, instead of taking pollen (left).

Insects that come looking for pollen and nectar can be threatened by predators like crab spiders. These little spiders hide in flowers and wait for prey. Their colors are often exactly the same as the colors of the flowers.

If a flower like this four o'clock (left) is not visited by pollinators, then it may be able to pollinate itself. As the flower wilts, its stamens and pistil curl up so that they come close together (below). This makes it possible for pollen from the anthers to reach the stigma.

Fruits and Seeds

Pollination is the beginning of a new stage in the life of a flowering plant. After the ovules in the ovary are fertilized by sperm, they begin to develop into seeds. Inside each seed is the tiny embryo of a new plant.

At the same time that the seeds are developing, the flower is changing. Its colors fade because they are no longer needed to attract pollinators. The petals soon fall off, and the other flower parts become dry and withered.

As the seeds grow, the ovary enlarges and its walls become thicker. It is developing into a **fruit**, the part of a plant that encloses and protects the seeds.

Once the seeds are fully developed, it is time for them to be released from the parent plant. In many plants, the fruit splits open and the seeds drop out on the ground. Some flowering plants, for example, the jewelweed or touch-me-not, shoot their seeds out.

Once they are released, some seeds, like those of the dandelion, fly away on the wind to places where they can grow. Other seeds depend on animals to disperse them. Birds eat berries and other fruits and drop the seeds on the ground. Insects such as ants also help to distribute the seeds of flowering plants. Just as insects play a vital role in pollination, so they also help to make sure that seeds will eventually grow into new plants.

After a corydalis flower is pollinated (above) and fertilized, seeds develop in its ovary. The seeds are scattered when the dried ovary bursts open (below).

57

An ant collecting corydalis seeds to take to its nest. Ants feed on the soft, white parts of the seeds and discard the rest. By dispersing the seeds, the insects help new corydalis plants to grow.

Glossary

angiosperms (AN-jee-uh-spurms)—plants with covered or enclosed seeds. All flowering plants are angiosperms.

anthers—the enlarged tips of stamens, where pollen is produced

anthocyanins (an-thoh-SI-uh-nins)—pigments that create blue, purple, and red colors in flowers

carotenes (KAR-uh-teens)—pigments that produce some of the yellow and orange colors in flowers. Carotenes also play a role in the food-making process of photosynthesis.

chlorophyll (KLOR-uh-fil)—a green pigment that absorbs sunlight, producing the energy that makes photosynthesis possible

chloroplasts (KLOR-uh-plasts)—tiny bodies (plastids) in plant cells that contain chlorophyll and carotenes

chromoplasts (KROM-uh-plasts)—tiny bodies (plastids) in plant cells that contain carotenes and related pigments

composite flower—a flower made up of many small flowers, or florets. The daisy, groundsel, and many other composite flowers have both tube florets and ray florets. Other composite flowers, for example, the thistle, have only tube florets.

cones—the structures on conifers that produce reproductive cells

conifers (KAHN-ih-fuhrs)—plants like pines and spruce that reproduce by means of cones

cross-pollination—the transfer of pollen from the stamens of one flower to the pistil of a similar flower on a different plant

cytoplasm (SIT-uh-plas-uhm)—the part of a cell where food-making and many other important processes take place

egg cells—female reproductive cells

electromagnetic radiation—energy that comes from the sun and travels through space in waves. Visible light is one of the forms of electromagnetic radiation.

embryo (EM-bree-oh)—a young plant or animal in an early stage of development

fertilization—the union of male sperm and female egg cells

filament—the thin stalk that forms the lower section of a stamen

floret—one of the small individual flowers that make up a composite flower

fruit—the part of a plant that encloses and protects seeds

gymnosperms (JIM-nih-spurms)—plants that produce naked seeds. Conifers like spruce and pines belong to this group.

keel—a flower structure formed by two petals that are joined and that enclose the reproductive parts. Keels are found in flowers of the pea family.

nectar guides—marks or patterns on flower petals that indicate the location of the nectaries

nectaries—the parts of flowers that contain nectar

ovary—the hollow chamber at the base of the pistil where seeds are formed

ovules (AHV-yuls)—tiny structures in a flower ovary that contain egg cells and can develop into seeds

petals—the colored parts of flowers that surround the reproductive organs

photosynthesis (fot-oh-SIN-thih-sis)—the process by which green plants use the energy of the sun to make food

pigments—natural coloring materials in plants and other living things. Pigments create colors by absorbing some wavelengths of light and reflecting others.

pistil—the female reproductive organ of a flower

pistillate (PIS-tih-late)—having a pistil but no stamens

plastids (PLAS-tihds)—tiny bodies in plant cells that contain chlorophyll and other pigments

pollen—a powdery substance produced by stamens that contains sperm

pollination—the transfer of pollen from stamens to pistil

pollinia (poh-LIN-ee-uh)—clusters of pollen grains found in orchids. The singular form of the word is **pollinium.**

proboscis (pro-BAS-uhs)—a tube-like extension of an insect's mouth

receptive—the condition of a pistil capable of receiving pollen

seed—the structure that develops from an ovule and contains a plant embryo

self-pollination—the transfer of pollen from the stamens to the pistil of the same flower or of another flower on the same plant

sepals (SEEP-uhls)—small, leaf-like structures at the base of a flower. Most sepals are green, but some are the same colors as the flower petals.

sexual reproduction—a form of reproduction in which a new individual is created through the union of male and female reproductive cells

sperm—male reproductive cells

spores (SPORS)—small bodies that are produced during one of the stages in the reproductive process of ferns, horsetails, and club mosses. Spores develop into

plants that produce male and female reproductive cells.

spurs—hollow extensions of petals or sepals that often enclose a flower's nectaries

stamens (STAY-muhns)—the male reproductive organs of flowers

staminate (STAM-ih-nate)—having stamens but no pistil

stigma—the sticky tip of a pistil

style—the stalk that connects the stigma to the ovary

ultraviolet light—short waves of electromagnetic radiation that lie beyond the violet end of the human visible light spectrum. Bees and some other insects can see ultraviolet light.

vegetative propagation—a form of reproduction in which a new plant develops from part of an existing plant

visible light spectrum—the range of electromagnetic radiation to which human eyes are sensitive

xanthophylls (ZAN-thih-fils)—pigments closely related to the carotenes that produce some of the yellow and orange colors of plants

Index

Pages listed in **bold** type include photographs of plants. Scientific names of plants are given in parentheses.

In studying crab spiders, photographer Yuko Sato discovered that some of the little predators did not blend in with the colors of the flowers in which they were hiding (left). When he took ultra-violet photographs of the flowers, Sato found that the spiders were concealed by patterns invisible to human eyes (right).

Photographer **Yuko Sato** first became interested in flower colors when he was studying and photographing crab spiders. Many of these small spiders match the colors of the flowers in which they hide while waiting for prey. After observing this surprising partnership, Sato began to investigate the complex subject of flower colors and the roles they play. The result is the collection of beautiful photographs featured in *Roses Red, Violets Blue*.

Author **Sylvia A. Johnson** is a writer and editor whose career has given her the opportunity to learn about many fascinating areas of science. Her books deal with subjects ranging from wolves and dinosaurs to beetles and coral reefs. In creating a text to accompany Yuko Sato's outstanding photographs, Johnson worked with specialists in botany while taking a closer look at the flowers growing in her own garden.